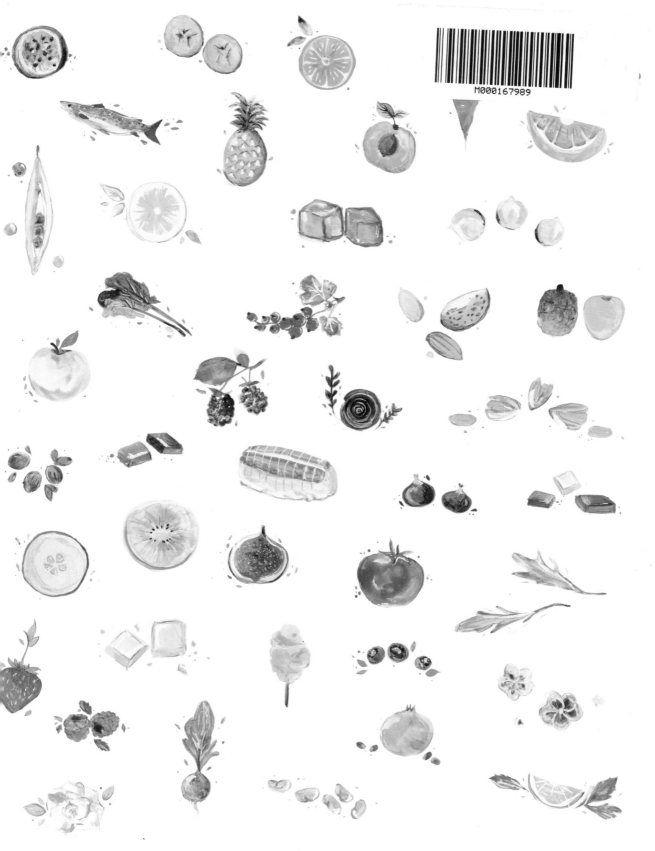

RAINBOW
TARTS

Emilie Guelpa

hardie grant books
MELBOURNE · LONDON

I dedicate this book to all lovers of colour, lovers of food and lovers of graphic design; but also to all of those who appreciate the good things in life!

SUMMARY

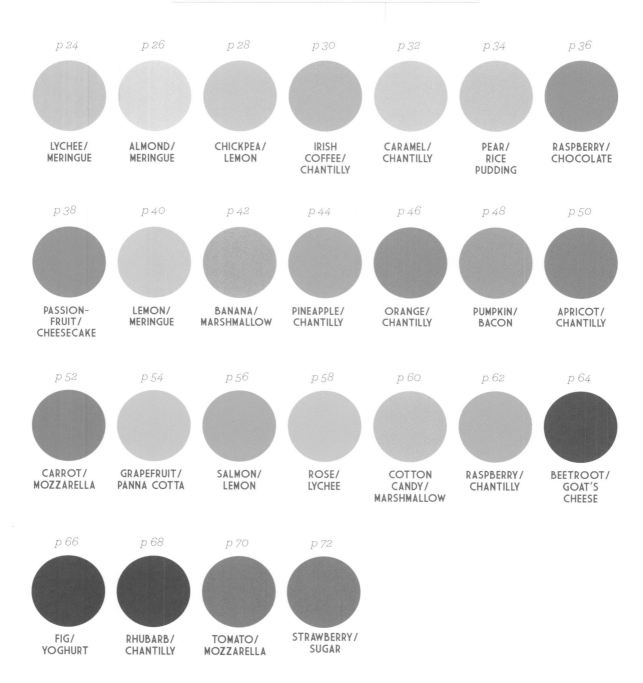

p 24
LYCHEE/
MERINGUE

p 26
ALMOND/
MERINGUE

p 28
CHICKPEA/
LEMON

p 30
IRISH
COFFEE/
CHANTILLY

p 32
CARAMEL/
CHANTILLY

p 34
PEAR/
RICE
PUDDING

p 36
RASPBERRY/
CHOCOLATE

p 38
PASSION-
FRUIT/
CHEESECAKE

p 40
LEMON/
MERINGUE

p 42
BANANA/
MARSHMALLOW

p 44
PINEAPPLE/
CHANTILLY

p 46
ORANGE/
CHANTILLY

p 48
PUMPKIN/
BACON

p 50
APRICOT/
CHANTILLY

p 52
CARROT/
MOZZARELLA

p 54
GRAPEFRUIT/
PANNA COTTA

p 56
SALMON/
LEMON

p 58
ROSE/
LYCHEE

p 60
COTTON
CANDY/
MARSHMALLOW

p 62
RASPBERRY/
CHANTILLY

p 64
BEETROOT/
GOAT'S
CHEESE

p 66
FIG/
YOGHURT

p 68
RHUBARB/
CHANTILLY

p 70
TOMATO/
MOZZARELLA

p 72
STRAWBERRY/
SUGAR

SUMMARY

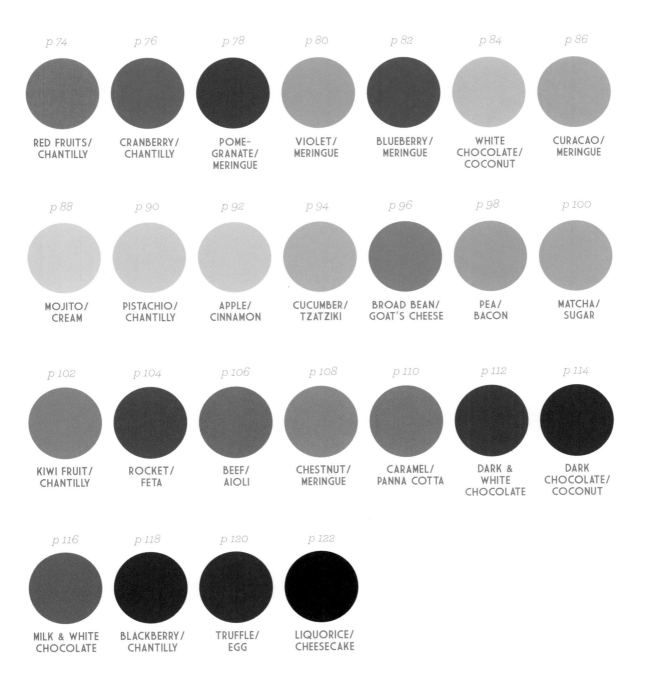

p 74 — RED FRUITS/ CHANTILLY

p 76 — CRANBERRY/ CHANTILLY

p 78 — POME- GRANATE/ MERINGUE

p 80 — VIOLET/ MERINGUE

p 82 — BLUEBERRY/ MERINGUE

p 84 — WHITE CHOCOLATE/ COCONUT

p 86 — CURACAO/ MERINGUE

p 88 — MOJITO/ CREAM

p 90 — PISTACHIO/ CHANTILLY

p 92 — APPLE/ CINNAMON

p 94 — CUCUMBER/ TZATZIKI

p 96 — BROAD BEAN/ GOAT'S CHEESE

p 98 — PEA/ BACON

p 100 — MATCHA/ SUGAR

p 102 — KIWI FRUIT/ CHANTILLY

p 104 — ROCKET/ FETA

p 106 — BEEF/ AIOLI

p 108 — CHESTNUT/ MERINGUE

p 110 — CARAMEL/ PANNA COTTA

p 112 — DARK & WHITE CHOCOLATE

p 114 — DARK CHOCOLATE/ COCONUT

p 116 — MILK & WHITE CHOCOLATE

p 118 — BLACKBERRY/ CHANTILLY

p 120 — TRUFFLE/ EGG

p 122 — LIQUORICE/ CHEESECAKE

INTRODUCTION

THE BEGINNING

In 2012, while I was arranging a set of colour-coded origami papers, something clicked: the desire to make a series of colourful tarts which would form a beautiful array of colour: a culinary palette. As a graphic designer, I use swatches every day for reference and to be inspired by the colours and shades. It was obvious that the swatch was the ideal form for my project!

I created a small series of tarts for the magazine *Fricote* and a book was the next natural step. 50 new colours, 50 shades, 50 recipes! A beautiful combination of colour, design and delicious food.

After many months of drawing, note-taking, painting and photographing; testing flavours and recipes with fruits, vegetables, and any other colourful ingredients I could find; arranging and rearranging colours and shades, here are my 50 recipes inspired by colours.

Bon appétit!

Emilie Guelpa

SOME TIPS BEFORE YOU START

There are so many different foods that can be used to create colour-inspired tarts. Feel free to make your own creations using fruits, vegetables, candy – or anything else you can think of. You can also use food dyes to achieve the different colours with more or less intensity. The important thing is to combine a white base at the bottom with a (more-or-less uniform) colour at the top.

To get the best results when whipping cream, it is important that the cream is very cold, and it's also a good idea to place the bowl and beaters in the refrigerator for at least 30 minutes before use. Ensuring that everything is chilled helps to create the lightest, fluffiest whipped cream, that holds its shape for longer. It's preferable to use an electric mixer, as this makes it much easier to beat the cream until it is nice and firm.

The recipes in this book are given for two tarts of approximately 11 cm × 14 cm (4¼ in × 5½ in). If you don't have a baking tin that is the correct size, you can use a larger tin and make an aluminium foil lining to adjust the size. When cutting pastry to size, you might like to cut a piece of cardboard to use as a template (cut pastry a little larger than the desired size, as it will shrink while cooking).

All of the flour used in the recipes is plain (all-purpose) flour, unless otherwise specified.

Pistachio paste is available from gourmet food stores. To make your own, blend a handful of skinned, unsalted pistachios with a pinch of sugar in a food processor. Add a few drops of olive oil and blend until the mixture is very smooth.

Brick pastry is a very thin Tunisian pastry, also known as 'brik'. If unavailable, you can substitute filo pastry, but use 4 sheets instead of 2. Cut the pastry into rectangles, brush with melted butter and layer the pastry so that you have 2 stacks of 4 rectangles. Bake for 3–4 minutes at 160°C (320°F) or until crisp and golden.

1 tablespoon is equivalent to 4 teaspoons.

Finally, the most important thing is to have fun! The kitchen should be a place of sharing, experimentation and relaxation. Don't hold back: be creative and express yourself!

BASIC RECIPES

CHOCOLATE SHORTCRUST
chocolate + vanilla + ground almonds

SALTED HAZELNUT
ground hazelnuts + butter + flour + salt

SHORTCRUST
vanilla + butter + flour + sugar

SALTED PARMESAN
parmesan + butter + flour

PASTRIES

Chocolate shortcrust pastry

1 egg | 40 g (1½ oz) icing (confectioners') sugar | 15 g (½ oz) ground almonds | 180 g (6½ oz) flour
1 teaspoon baking powder | 100 g (3½ oz) unsalted butter, coarsely chopped into small pieces
10 g (¼ oz) unsweetened cocoa powder | a few drops of natural vanilla extract | pinch of sea salt

Line a tray with baking paper. In a mixing bowl, beat together the egg and sugar. Add the ground almonds, flour, baking powder, butter, cocoa, vanilla and salt, and roughly combine using your hands. Tip onto a floured work surface and knead the dough until it is smooth and forms a ball. Add a little flour if the dough sticks. Roll the dough and cut into four 12 cm × 15 cm (4¾ in × 6 in) rectangles. Place onto the prepared tray, prick with a fork and then chill for 30 minutes. Preheat oven to 180°C (350°F). Bake for 15–20 minutes, or until lightly golden.

Salted hazelnut pastry

100 g (3½ oz) flour | 30 g (1 oz) ground hazelnuts | pinch of salt | 1 egg | 1 egg yolk
100 g (3½ oz) unsalted butter, coarsely chopped into small pieces

Line a tray with baking paper. In a mixing bowl, combine the flour, ground hazelnuts and salt. Add the egg and egg yolk, and butter, and roughly combine using your hands. Tip onto a floured work surface and knead the dough until it is smooth and forms a ball. Add a little flour if the dough sticks. Roll the dough and cut into two 13 cm × 16 cm (5 in × 6¼ in) rectangles. Trim about 1 cm (½ in) from each edge and use these strips to make a border around the edge of the rectangle. Place onto the prepared tray, prick with a fork and then chill for 30 minutes. Preheat oven to 180°C (350°F). Bake for 10–15 minutes, or until lightly golden.

Shortcrust pastry

160 g (5½ oz) flour | 25 g (1 oz) icing (confectioners') sugar | 50 g (1¾ oz) unsalted butter, coarsely chopped into small pieces | pinch of sea salt |1 vanilla bean | 1 egg | 3 tablespoons milk

Line a tray with baking paper. Combine the flour, sugar, butter and salt in a mixing bowl. Cut the vanilla bean lengthways, and scrape the seeds into the bowl using the tip of the knife. Add the egg and milk, and roughly combine using your hands. Tip onto a floured work surface and knead the dough until it is smooth and forms a ball. Add a little flour if the dough sticks. Roll the dough and cut into four 12 cm × 15 cm (4¾ in × 6 in) rectangles. Place onto the prepared tray, prick with a fork and then chill for 30 minutes. Preheat oven to 180°C (350°F). Bake for 20 minutes, or until lightly golden.

Salted parmesan pastry

160 g (5½ oz) flour | 70 g (2½ oz) parmesan, finely grated | pinch of salt | 1 egg
100 g (3½ oz) unsalted butter, coarsely chopped into small pieces

Line a tray with baking paper. In a mixing bowl, combine the flour, parmesan and salt. Add the egg and butter, and combine using your hands. Tip onto a floured work surface and knead the dough until it is smooth and forms a ball. Add a little flour if the dough sticks. Roll the dough and cut into two 12 cm × 15 cm (4¾ in × 6 in) rectangles. Place onto the prepared tray, prick with a fork and then chill for 30 minutes. Preheat oven to 180°C (350°F). Bake for 10–15 minutes, or until lightly golden.

ROYAL ICING

sugar + water

CHANTILLY

cream + sugar

CHOCOLATE

white chocolate + cream

ITALIAN MERINGUE

egg whites + sugar syrup

RICE PUDDING

round rice + hot milk

CREAM

fresh cream

COCONUT

coconut + cream

FRENCH MERINGUE

egg whites + sugar

MASCARPONE

mascarpone + sugar

CREAMS

Chantilly cream

250 ml (8½ fl oz) chilled cream | 20 g (¾ oz) icing (confectioners') sugar

Beat the cream using an electric mixer until firm peaks form. Sift the sugar into the cream and beat for a further few seconds until the sugar is well incorporated.

Italian meringue

100 g (3½ oz) caster (superfine) sugar | 1 egg white

Heat the sugar with 50 ml (1¾ fl oz) water over high heat for about 10 minutes, or until the mixture is syrupy and has reduced by half. Remove from the heat and set aside. Beat the egg white using an electric mixer. When the white is firm, add the syrup in a thin stream while still beating. Beat until well combined and the meringue is smooth and glossy.

French meringue

1 egg white | 35 g (1¼ oz) caster (superfine) sugar | 40 g (1½ oz) icing (confectioners') sugar

Preheat oven to 80°C (175°F). Line a tray with baking paper. Beat the egg white using an electric mixer. When the white has started to become fluffy and opaque, sprinkle in the caster sugar. Continue beating until stiff peaks form. Using a spatula, gently fold in the icing sugar, lifting the egg white in the same direction as you fold. Form two 12 cm × 15 cm (4¾ in × 6 in) rectangles of meringue on the tray, smoothing the edges and the top with a spatula. Bake for 2 hours, or until the meringue lifts easily from the baking paper.

Panna cotta

90 g (3¼ oz) caster (superfine) sugar | 400 ml (13½ fl oz) cream | 400 ml (13½ fl oz) milk
1 teaspoon gelatine powder | 1 vanilla bean

Combine the sugar, cream, milk and gelatine in a saucepan over medium–high heat. Cut the vanilla bean lengthways, and scrape out the seeds using the tip of the knife. Add the seeds and the bean to the saucepan. Bring to the boil and simmer for 30 seconds. Remove from the heat and pour into a deep tray that is at least 15 cm × 24 cm (6 in × 9½ in). Refrigerate for at least 3 hours or until set. When the panna cotta is set, turn out onto a flat surface and, using a hot knife, carefully cut into two 11 cm × 14 cm (4¼ in × 5½ in) rectangles.

CULINARY PALETTE

WHITE

lychee, almond, coconut, scallop, feta, leek,
white chocolate, cream, yoghurt, parsnip ...

BEIGE

peach, white sesame, mushroom,
pear, chickpea, foie gras ...

YELLOW

banana, lemon, pineapple,
mango, yellow tomato ...

ORANGE

apricot, pumpkin (winter squash),
papaya, carrot, sweet potato, orange ...

PINK

candy-striped beetroot, rhubarb, fig,
rose, grapefruit, cranberry, salmon ...

RED

raspberry, strawberry, redcurrant, apple,
tomato, capsicum (pepper), pomegranate ...

CULINARY PALETTE

PURPLE

lavender, violet, plum, blueberry,
beetroot, purple potato ...

BLUE

curaçao, candies,
blue cheese ...

GREEN

spinach, mint, matcha, peas, kiwi fruit, beans,
rocket (arugula), pistachio, cucumber ...

LIGHT BROWN

chestnut, caramel, milk chocolate,
cinnamon, date, hazelnut, nutmeg ...

BROWN

dark chocolate, coffee, tea, praline
dulce de leche ...

BLACK

blackberry, truffle, liquorice, squid ink,
black pudding, black sesame ...

RECIPES

LYCHEE – MERINGUE

Base 1 × quantity French meringue (page 19)

Colour topping 24 lychees, peeled and cored

White topping 150 ml (5 fl oz) cream

To make the base, follow the recipe for French meringue on page 19.

To make the white topping, beat the cream using electric beaters until stiff peaks form.

Spread the cream onto the meringue and arrange the lychees on top.

ALMOND – MERINGUE

Base 1 × quantity French meringue (page 19)

Colour topping 50 g (1¾ oz) blanched almonds

White topping 150 ml (5 fl oz) cream
2 teaspoons icing (confectioners') sugar

To make the base, follow the recipe for French meringue on page 19.

To make the white topping, beat the cream using electric beaters until firm peaks form. Add the sugar and beat for a further few seconds until the sugar is well incorporated.

Spread the cream onto the meringue and arrange the almonds on top. If desired, serve with an orange and passionfruit coulis or red fruits.

CHICKPEA – LEMON

Base 50 g (1¾ oz) flour | 20 g (¾ oz) cornflour (cornstarch) | salt
2 teaspoons baking powder | 200 g (7 oz) Greek-style yoghurt
40 g (1½ oz) thick (double/heavy) cream | 2 egg whites | olive oil

Colour topping 250 g (9 oz) tinned chickpeas (garbanzo beans)
juice of 1 lemon | 120 ml (4 fl oz) olive oil
2 pinches sweet paprika | salt | pepper

White topping 2 tablespoons thick (double/heavy) cream
a few drops of lemon juice

To prepare the blinis base, combine the flour, cornflour, salt and baking powder in a bowl. Make a well in the middle and pour in 4 tablespoons warm water. Add the yoghurt and cream, and mix well. Beat the egg whites until soft peaks form and fold gently into the mixture. Cover with plastic wrap and refrigerate for 1 hour.

To make the colour topping, drain the chickpeas, place them in a food processor and pulse, adding the lemon juice little by little. Add the olive oil, paprika, salt and pepper, and process until completely smooth, adding a little more oil or lemon juice if necessary.

To make the white topping, beat the cream and lemon juice together using an electric mixer until firm peaks form.

Heat a little olive oil in a frying pan over medium–high heat. Place a 11 cm × 14 cm (4¼ in × 5½ in) rectangular cookie cutter in the pan and pour half the batter in. Cook for 3–5 minutes, or until bubbles appear on the surface and the bottom is well browned, and then turn and cook for another 3–5 minutes. Repeat with the remaining batter.

Spread the chickpea purée onto the upper part of the base and the cream onto the lower part.

IRISH COFFEE – CHANTILLY

Base 50 g (1¾ oz) unsalted butter, softened
80 g (2¾ oz) flour | 70 g (2½ oz) sugar | 4 tablespoons whisky

Colour topping 30 g (1 oz) sugar | ¼ teaspoon gelatine powder
100 ml (3½ fl oz) espresso coffee | 150 ml (5 fl oz) cream

White topping 100 ml (3½ fl oz) cream
1 tablespoon icing (confectioners') sugar

To make the crumble base, preheat oven to 180°C (350°F). Line a tray with baking paper. Combine the butter, flour and sugar. Add the whisky and then coarsely mix with your hands to make a crumble. Spread the crumble onto the prepared tray and bake for 15 minutes, or until browned.

To make the colour topping, combine the sugar, gelatine and coffee in a small saucepan over medium heat. Bring to the boil for 30 seconds then set aside to cool. Beat the cream until stiff peaks form. Add the coffee mixture and mix gently until well combined. Transfer to a piping bag and refrigerate until needed.

To make the white topping, beat the cream using an electric mixer until firm peaks form. Add the sugar and beat for a further few seconds until the sugar is well incorporated. Transfer to a piping bag.

On serving plates, form the baked crumble into two 11 cm × 14 cm (4¼ in × 5½ in) rectangles. Pipe the coffee mixture onto the upper part of the rectangle, and pipe the cream onto the lower part.

CARAMEL – CHANTILLY

Base 1 × quantity Shortcrust pastry (page 17)

Colour topping 100 g (3½ oz) sugar | 50 g (1¾ oz) unsalted butter
250 ml (8½ fl oz) chilled cream | a pinch of sea salt

White topping 100 ml (3½ fl oz) cream
1 tablespoon icing (confectioners') sugar

To make the base, follow the recipe for Shortcrust pastry on page 17.

To make the colour topping, place the sugar in a heavy-based saucepan over medium–high and heat until the sugar starts to brown. When it is well coloured, add the butter and 100 ml (3½ fl oz) of the cream. Stir with a wooden spoon for 3–4 minutes then remove from the heat. Add salt and set aside until completely cool. Beat the remaining cream using an electric mixer until firm peaks form. Gently fold the cooled caramel into the cream and refrigerate for at least 2 hours. Transfer to a piping bag and refrigerate until needed.

To make the white topping, beat the cream using an electric mixer until firm peaks form. Sift the sugar into the cream and beat for a further few seconds until the sugar is well incorporated. Transfer to a piping bag.

Pipe the caramel onto the upper part of the pastry and the cream onto the lower part.

PEAR – RICE PUDDING

Base 500 ml (17 fl oz) milk | 20 g (¾ oz) sugar
1 vanilla bean | 90 g (3¼ oz) short-grain rice

Colour topping 2 pears | 20 g (¾ oz) sugar

To make the rice pudding base, place the milk and sugar in a heavy-based saucepan over medium–high heat. Cut the vanilla bean lengthways, and scrape out the seeds using the tip of the knife. Add the seeds and the bean to the milk. When the milk is hot, reduce the heat, add the rice and cook for about 20 minutes, stirring occasionally, until the rice is tender. Remove the vanilla bean and transfer the rice to a bowl. Set aside to cool completely.

To make the colour topping, cut the pears into small cubes.

On serving plates, form the rice pudding into two 11 cm × 14 cm (4¼ in × 5½ in) rectangles. Arrange the pears on the upper part of the rectangles and sprinkle with sugar.

RASPBERRY – CHOCOLATE

Base ½ × quantity Chocolate shortcrust pastry (page 17)

Colour topping 90 g (3 oz) dark chocolate | 3 eggs, separated
250 g (9 oz) raspberries | edible gold dust, for decorating

White topping 150 ml (5 fl oz) cream
1 tablespoon icing (confectioners') sugar

To make the base, follow the recipe for Chocolate shortcrust pastry on page 17.

To make the colour topping, place the chocolate in a heatproof bowl placed over a large saucepan of simmering water. Stir occasionally until the chocolate has completely melted. Remove from the heat and mix in the egg yolks. Beat the egg whites using an electric mixer until firm. Gently fold the egg whites into the chocolate mixture. Transfer to a piping bag and refrigerate for at least 1 hour. Cover the raspberries in gold dust using a soft paintbrush.

To make the white topping, beat the cream using an electric mixer until firm peaks form. Sift the sugar into the cream and beat for a further few seconds until the sugar is well incorporated. Transfer to a piping bag.

Pipe the chocolate mousse onto the upper part of the base and arrange the raspberries on top. Pipe the cream onto the lower part and serve.

PASSIONFRUIT – CHEESECAKE

Base 100 g (3½ oz) sweet spiced biscuits (cookies)
80 g (2¾ oz) unsalted butter

Colour topping pulp from 5 large passionfruit
50 g (1¾ oz) caster (superfine) sugar

White topping 300 g (10½ oz) cream cheese | 250 g (9 oz) mascarpone
150 g (5½ oz) caster (superfine) sugar | 4 eggs

To make the biscuit base, crush the biscuits into very small pieces and put into a mixing bowl. Melt the butter and mix into the crushed biscuits. Line a small baking tin with baking paper and spread the biscuits over the base of the tin. Refrigerate for at least 1 hour.

To make the white topping, preheat oven to 160°C (320°F). Combine the cream cheese, mascarpone, sugar and eggs using an electric mixer. Pour over the chilled biscuit base and then bake for 50 minutes. Remove from the oven and allow to cool completely.

To make the coloured topping, combine the passionfruit and sugar.

Cut the cheesecake into two 11 cm × 14 cm (4¼ in × 5½ in) rectangles. Spread the sweetened passionfruit pulp onto the upper part of the rectangles and serve.

LEMON – MERINGUE

Base 1 × quantity Shortcrust pastry (page 17)
finely grated zest of 1 bergamot orange or orange

Colour topping 100 g (3½ oz) caster (superfine) sugar
5 egg yolks | juice and finely grated zest of 4 lemons
500 ml (17 fl oz) milk | 50 g (1¾ oz) cornflour (cornstarch)

White topping 1 × quantity Italian meringue (page 19)

To make the base, follow the recipe for Shortcrust pastry on page 17, replacing the vanilla bean with the bergamot orange or orange zest.

To make the colour topping, whisk together the sugar and egg yolks. Transfer to a saucepan over medium–high heat and add the lemon juice, milk and half the zest. When the mixture is hot, add the cornflour and stir continuously until the mixture thickens. Remove from the heat and allow to cool completely. Transfer to a piping bag and refrigerate until needed.

To make the white topping, follow the recipe for Italian meringue on page 19 then transfer to a piping bag.

Pipe the lemon onto the upper part of the pastry and the meringue onto the lower part. Sprinkle the lemon with the remaining lemon zest. If desired, lightly brown the meringue with a small blowtorch before serving.

BANANA – MARSHMALLOW

Base 2 sheets brick (Tunisian) pastry (see p 13)
10 g (¼ oz) unsalted butter, melted

Colour topping 25 g (1 oz) sugar | 3 bananas, thickly sliced
coloured sugar or grated white chocolate, to decorate

White topping 10 marshmallows

To make the base, preheat oven to 180°C (350°F) and line a tray with baking paper. Cut the pastry into four 11 cm × 14 cm (4¼ in × 5½ in) rectangles. Place onto the prepared tray and brush with melted butter. Bake for 3–4 minutes, or until the pastry is golden.

To make the colour topping, heat the sugar in a heavy-based pan over medium–high heat. Once the sugar starts to colour, add the banana and cook for 1–2 minutes, or until tender and caramelised.

To make the white topping, place the marshmallows and 50 ml (1¾ fl oz) water in a mixing bowl placed over a large saucepan of simmering water. Stir occasionally until the marshmallows have melted and the mixture is cooled. Remove from the heat and set aside to cool for a few minutes (do not leave too long or else the mixture will become too hard).

On serving plates, stack two sheets of pastry on each plate. Arrange the banana on the upper part of the pastry and spread the marshmallow on the lower part. Sprinkle with coloured sugar or a little grated white chocolate.

PINEAPPLE – CHANTILLY

Base 1 × quantity Shortcrust pastry (page 17)

Colour topping 1 small pineapple
20 g (¾ oz) icing (confectioners') sugar

White topping 1 × quantity Chantilly cream (page 19)

To make the base, follow the recipe for Shortcrust pastry on page 17.

To make the colour topping, preheat oven to 180°C (350°F) and line a tray with baking paper. Remove the top of the pineapple and, using a mandoline or a sharp knife, cut 10 thin slices of pineapple. Arrange the slices on the prepared tray and sprinkle with the icing sugar. Cover with another sheet of baking paper and pour some rice or baking weights over the top to hold the paper down. Cook for 30 minutes, or until the pineapple is well caramelised. Meanwhile, cut the skin off the remaining pineapple and cut the flesh into small cubes.

To make the white topping, follow the recipe for Chantilly cream on page 19.

Spread the cream over the pastry. Arrange the pineapple cubes on the upper part and then place the candied slices over the top.

ORANGE – CHANTILLY

Base 1 × quantity Shortcrust pastry (page 17)
finely grated zest of 1 orange

Colour topping 3 oranges | 20 g (¾ oz) icing (confectioners') sugar
100 g (3½ oz) caster (superfine) sugar | 5 egg yolks
500 ml (17 fl oz) milk | 50 g (1¾ oz) cornflour (cornstarch)

White topping 1 × quantity Chantilly cream (page 19)

To make the base, follow the recipe for Shortcrust pastry on page 17, replacing the vanilla bean with the orange zest.

To make the colour topping, preheat oven to 180°C (350°F) and line a tray with baking paper. Cut two of the oranges into very thin slices. Arrange the slices on the prepared tray and sprinkle with the icing sugar. Cover with another sheet of baking paper and pour some rice or baking weights over the top to hold the paper down. Cook for 30 minutes, or until the orange is well caramelised. Meanwhile, squeeze the juice from the remaining orange. Whisk together the caster sugar and egg yolks. Transfer to a saucepan over medium–high heat and add the milk and orange juice. When the mixture is hot, add the cornflour and stir continuously until the mixture thickens. Remove from the heat and allow to cool completely.

To make the white topping, follow the recipe for Chantilly cream on page 19.

Spread the orange cream onto the upper part of the pastry and the Chantilly cream onto the lower part. Arrange the candied oranges on top of the orange cream and serve.

PUMPKIN – BACON

Base 1 quantity Salted hazelnut pastry (page 17)

Colour topping 500 g (1 lb 2 oz) butternut pumpkin (squash)
20 g (¾ oz) butter | 10 g (¼ oz) parmesan | 1 tablespoon cream
1 egg | 1 tablespoon flour | 1 teaspoon sugar
salt and ground black pepper

White topping 70 g (2½ oz) bacon | 150 ml (5 fl oz) cream

To make prepare the white topping, cook the bacon in a frying pan over medium–high heat then drain on paper towel. Place the bacon with the cream in a saucepan and heat for 5 minutes on low. Set aside to cool completely, then refrigerate for two hours.

To make the base, follow the recipe for Salted hazelnut pastry on page 17.

To make the colour topping, chop the pumkin into chunks and boil in lightly salted water for about 15 minutes, or until tender. Drain and then mash the pumpkin using a potato masher. Press the pumpkin mash through a fine-mesh sieve to make it smooth. Stir in the butter, parmesan, cream, egg, flour, sugar, and salt and pepper. Pour the pumpkin mixture onto the pastry base and then bake for 20 minutes. Remove from the oven and allow to cool for 5 minutes.

Meanwhile, strain the bacon cream and discard the bacon. Beat the cream using an electric mixer until firm peaks form. Spread the cream over the lower part of the pumpkin tart and serve.

APRICOT – CHANTILLY

Base 1 × quantity Shortcrust pastry (page 17)

Colour topping 70 g (2½ oz) icing (confectioners') sugar
70 g (2½ oz) unsalted butter, diced | 70 g (2½ oz) ground almonds
7 apricots, sliced | 25 g (1 oz) sugar
15 g (½ oz) toasted almonds, roughly chopped

White topping 150 ml (5 fl oz) chilled cream
1 tablespoon icing (confectioners') sugar

To make the base, follow the recipe for Shortcrust pastry on page 17, but do not bake. Preheat oven to 180°C (350°F).

To make the colour topping, mix the icing sugar, butter and ground almonds using an electric mixer until smooth. Spread the mixture onto the upper part of the chilled pastry and arrange the apricot slices on top. Sprinkle with the sugar (use a little more if your apricots aren't very sweet) and top with the chopped almonds. Bake for 20 minutes then set aside to cool.

To make the white topping, beat the cream using an electric mixer until firm peaks form. Sift the sugar into the cream and beat for a further few seconds until the sugar is well incorporated.

Spread the cream over the lower part of the apricot tart and serve.

CARROT – MOZZARELLA

Base 1 × quantity Salted parmesan pastry (page 17)

Colour topping 5 carrots, peeled and cut into triangles
30 g (1 oz) butter | pinch of turmeric
salt and ground black pepper | sesame seeds, to decorate

White topping 25 ml (¾ fl oz) cream
100 g (3½ oz) fresh mozzarella, roughly chopped
50 g (1¾ oz) mascarpone | salt and ground black pepper

To make the base, follow the recipe for Salted parmesan pastry on page 17.

To make the white topping, combine the cream and mozzarella in a saucepan over low heat. Stir occasionally until the mozzarella has melted. Remove from the heat, stir in the mascarpone and season with salt and pepper. Set aside to cool completely then refrigerate for 30 minutes, or until the cream has thickened.

To make the colour topping, boil the carrots in lightly salted water for about 8 minutes until just tender. Drain. Melt the butter in a frying pan over medium–high heat. Add the carrots, turmeric, and salt and pepper and sauté for 5–6 minutes.

Arrange the carrots on the upper part of the pastry and spread the mozzarella cream onto the lower part. Sprinkle with sesame seeds and serve.

GRAPEFRUIT – PANNA COTTA

Base 1 × quantity Panna cotta (page 19)

Colour topping 2 pink grapefruit
1½ teaspoons gelatine powder
30 g (1 oz) sugar, plus extra if required

To make the base, follow the recipe for Panna cotta on page 19.

To make the colour topping, juice one grapefruit, and peel and segment the other, removing the outer membrane. Set the peeled grapefruit aside in the refrigerator. Combine the juice with the sugar and gelatine in a saucepan over high heat and bring to the boil. Remove from the heat and immediately pour into a deep tray that is at least 11 cm × 22 cm (4¼ in × 8¾ in), so that the liquid is about 3 mm (⅛ in) deep. Refrigerate for at least 1 hour, or until set.

Unmould the grapefruit jelly and cut into squares. Place carefully onto the upper half of the panna cotta and decorate with pieces from the grapefruit segments. Sprinkle with a little extra sugar if the grapefruit is very tart.

SALMON – LEMON

Base 50 g (1¾ oz) flour | 20 g (¾ oz) cornflour (cornstarch) | salt
2 teaspoons baking powder | 200 g (7 oz) Greek-style yoghurt
40 g (1½ oz) thick (double/heavy) cream
2 egg whites | olive oil

Colour topping 150 g (5½ oz) smoked salmon

White topping 2 tablespoons crème fraîche or sour cream
a few drops of lemon juice

To prepare the blinis base, combine the flour, cornflour, salt and baking powder in a bowl. Make a well in the middle and pour in 4 tablespoons warm water. Add the yoghurt and cream, and mix well. Beat the egg whites until they form soft peaks and fold gently into the mixture. Cover with a plastic wrap and refrigerate for 1 hour.

To make the white topping, whisk the cream and lemon juice together.

Heat a little olive oil in a frying pan over medium–high heat. Place a 11 cm × 14 cm (4¼ in × 5½ in) rectangular cookie cutter in the pan and pour half the batter in. Cook for 3 minutes, or until bubbles appear on the surface and the bottom is well browned, and then turn and cook for another 2–3 minutes. Repeat with the remaining batter.

Arrange the salmon on the upper part of the base and spread the cream onto the lower part.

ROSE – LYCHEE

Base 100 g (3½ oz) unsalted butter | pinch of salt
1 teaspoon caster (superfine) sugar | 150 g (5½ oz) flour | 4 eggs

Colour topping 250 g (9 oz) fondant | red food dye
10 lychees, cut into small cubes

White topping 1 × quantity Chantilly cream (page 19)

To make the choux pastry base, preheat oven to 160°C (320°F) and line a tray with baking paper. Combine the butter, salt and sugar with 250 ml (8½ fl oz) water in a saucepan over medium–high heat and bring to the boil. Remove from the heat and add the flour in one go. Return to the heat and stir continuously until the dough forms a smooth ball that comes away from the edge of the saucepan. Transfer to a bowl. Add the eggs one by one, making sure to mix the dough thoroughly between each egg. Transfer the choux pastry into a large piping bag fitted with a wide nozzle and pipe two 11 cm × 14 cm (4¼ in × 5½ in) rectangles onto the prepared tray. With the remaining dough, pipe small balls onto the tray, then smooth the tops lightly with a fork dipped in water. Bake for 30–35 minutes, or until golden brown.

To make the white topping, follow the recipe for Chantilly cream on page 19 then transfer to a piping bag.

To make the colour topping, melt the fondant with a little red food dye to get a pink tint. Dip the tops of the choux pastries into the fondant and set aside to dry. Make slits in the bottom of the choux pastries using a sharp knife, then fill with the cream and a few cubes of lychee.

Arrange the filled choux pastries on the upper part of the rectangle base then pipe cream onto the lower part.

COTTON CANDY – MARSHMALLOW

Base 2 sheets brick (Tunisian) pastry (see p 13)
10 g (¼ oz) unsalted butter, melted

Colour topping 40 g (1½ oz) cotton candy

White topping 10 marshmallows

To make the base, preheat oven to 180°C (350°F) and line a tray with baking paper. Cut the pastry into four 11 cm × 14 cm (4¼ in × 5½ in) rectangles. Place onto the prepared tray and brush with butter. Bake for 3 minutes, or until the pastry is golden.

To make the white topping, place the marshmallows and 50 ml (1¾ fl oz) water in a mixing bowl placed over a large saucepan of simmering water. Stir occasionally until the marshmallows have melted and the mixture is cooled. Remove from the heat and set aside to cool for a few minutes (do not leave too long or else the mixture will become too hard).

On serving plates, stack two sheets of pastry on each plate. Arrange the cotton candy on the upper part of the pastry and spread the marshmallow on the lower part.

RASPBERRY – CHANTILLY

Base 1 × quantity Shortcrust pastry (page 17)

Colour topping 125 g (4½ oz) raspberries | 30 g (1 oz) sugar
¾ teaspoon gelatine powder | redcurrants, to decorate

White topping 1 × quantity Chantilly cream (page 19)

To make the base, follow the recipe for Shortcrust pastry on page 17.

To make the colour topping, combine the raspberries, sugar and gelatine with 20 ml (¾ fl oz) water in a saucepan over medium heat. Crush the fruit gently with a wooden spoon and bring to the boil. Remove from the heat and strain through a fine-mesh sieve to remove any seeds. Set aside to cool completely.

To make the white topping, follow the recipe for Chantilly cream on page 19. Transfer half the cream to a piping bag and set the remainder aside.

Gently fold the cooled raspberry liquid into the reserved cream, then spread onto the upper part of the base. Pipe the Chantilly cream onto the lower part and decorate with redcurrants.

BEETROOT – GOAT'S CHEESE

Base 1 × quantity Salted parmesan pastry (page 17)

Colour topping 1 beetroot (beet), peeled | 3 tablespoons olive oil
1 tablespoon balsamic vinegar | 1 teaspoon mustard
salt and ground black pepper

White topping 2 tablespoons crème fraîche or sour cream
80 g (2¾ oz) soft goat's cheese

To make the base, follow the recipe for Salted parmesan pastry on page 17.

To make the white topping, mash together the crème fraîche and the goat's cheese.

To make the colour topping, slice the beetroot very thinly using a mandoline or sharp knife. In a small bowl, combine the oil, vinegar, mustard, and salt and pepper to make a dressing.

Arrange the beetroot on the upper part of the base and spread the goat's cheese on the lower half. Serve with the dressing on the side.

FIG - YOGHURT

Base 1 × quantity Shortcrust pastry (page 17)

Colour topping 40 g (1½ oz) unsalted butter, chopped
40 g (1½ oz) icing (confectioners') sugar
40 g (1½ oz) ground almonds | 10 figs, peeled and sliced
5 tablespoons honey

White topping 100 g (3½ oz) Greek-style yoghurt
15 g (½ oz) icing (confectioners') sugar

To make the base, follow the recipe for Shortcrust pastry on page 17, but do not bake. Preheat oven to 180°C (350°F).

To make the white topping, mix together the yoghurt and sugar.

To make the colour topping, mix the butter, icing sugar and ground almonds using an electric mixer until smooth. Spread the mixture onto the upper part of the chilled pastry and arrange the fig slices on top. Drizzle with honey. Bake for 20 minutes then set aside to cool.

Spread the yoghurt on the lower half of the base and serve.

RHUBARB - CHANTILLY

Base 1 × quantity Shortcrust pastry (page 17)

Colour topping 250 g (9 oz) rhubarb, trimmed and chopped
30 g (1 oz) sugar | red food dye (optional)

White topping 150 ml (5 fl oz) chilled cream | 1 vanilla bean
10 g (¼ oz) icing (confectioners') sugar

To make the base, follow the recipe for Shortcrust pastry on page 17.

To make the colour topping, place the rhubarb in a small saucepan over medium heat. Add the sugar and 20 ml (¾ fl oz) water and simmer gently until the rhubarb breaks down. Taste for sweetness and add a little more sugar if the rhubarb is too acidic, and add a few drops of red food dye if the rhubarb needs a little more colour.

To make the white topping, place the cream into the bowl of an electric mixer. Cut the vanilla pod lengthways, and scrape the seeds into the bowl using the tip of the knife. Beat the cream until firm peaks form, then sift in the icing sugar and beat for a further few seconds until the sugar is well incorporated.

Spread the rhubarb on the upper part of the base and the cream onto the lower part.

TOMATO – MOZZARELLA

Base 1 × quantity Salted parmesan pastry (page 17)

Colour topping 12 cherry tomatoes, halved
olive oil, for drizzling | salt

White topping 100 g (3½ oz) fresh mozzarella, roughly chopped
25 ml (¾ fl oz) cream | 50 g (1¾ oz) mascarpone
salt and ground black pepper

To make the base, follow the recipe for Salted parmesan pastry on page 17.

To make the white topping, combine the mozzarella and cream in a saucepan over low heat. Stir occasionally until the mozzarella has melted. Remove from the heat, stir in the mascarpone and season with salt and pepper. Set aside to cool completely then refrigerate for 30 minutes, or until the cream has thickened.

To make the coloured topping, preheat oven to 180°C (350°F). Arrange the cherry tomatoes on a baking tray and drizzle with olive oil. Bake for 20 minutes, or until the tomatoes have caramelised.

Arrange the tomatoes on the upper part of the base and sprinkle with salt. Spread the mozzarella cream onto the lower part and serve.

STRAWBERRY - SUGAR

Base 1 × quantity Shortcrust pastry (page 17)

Colour topping | 1 tablespoon white balsamic vinegar
35 g (1¼ oz) caster (superfine) sugar | a few mint leaves
15 strawberries, trimmed and halved
80 g (2¾ oz) strawberry jam

White topping 70 g (2½ oz) icing (confectioners') sugar

To make the base, follow the recipe for Shortcrust pastry on page 17.

To make the white topping, mix the icing sugar with about 1 tablespoon of water (the mixture needs to be thick enough to not spread but not be too dense).

To make the colour topping, combine the vinegar, sugar and a few mint leaves in a small bowl. Add the strawberries and leave to marinate for 10 minutes.

Spread the strawberry jam onto the upper part of the base and arrange the marinated strawberries on top. Spread the sugar icing on the lower part and decorate with a few mint leaves.

RED FRUITS – CHANTILLY

Base 1 × quantity Shortcrust pastry (page 17)

Colour topping 5 tablespoons red-fruits jam
250 g (9 oz) raspberries | 200 g (7 oz) redcurrants

White topping 150 ml (5 fl oz) chilled cream
10 g (¼ oz) icing (confectioners') sugar

To make the base, follow the recipe for Shortcrust pastry on page 17.

To make the white topping, beat the cream using an electric mixer until firm peaks form. Sift the sugar into the cream and beat for a further few seconds until the sugar is well incorporated.

Spread the jam onto the upper part of the base and arrange the raspberries and redcurrants in an alternating pattern on top. Spread the cream on the lower part and serve.

CRANBERRY – CHANTILLY

Base 2 × quantity Shortcrust pastry (page 17) | red food dye

Colour topping 200 g (7 oz) cranberries, roughly chopped
150 g (5½ oz) sugar

White topping 1 × quantity Chantilly cream (page 19)

To make the base, follow the recipe for Shortcrust pastry on page 17, just until the dough has come together. Divide the dough into three portions. Roll out two portions of the dough and cut into 12 cm × 15 cm (4¾ in × 6 in) rectangles. Place onto the prepared tray and prick with a fork. To the remaining dough, add a few drops of food dye, and knead until the dough is evenly coloured. Roll out the red dough and cut into strips 1 cm (½ in) wide. Place onto the tray with the rectangles and refriegerate for 30 minutes. Preheat oven to 180°C (350°F).

To make the colour topping, combine the cranberries and sugar with 10 ml (¼ fl oz) water in a saucepan over low heat. Cook gently for 10 minutes, or until all of the water has evaporated. Spread the cranberries over the upper part of the chilled pastry and arrange the strips of red dough in a lattice over the top (you'll need to trim the strips to fit). Bake for 20 minutes, then remove from the oven and allow to cool.

To make the white topping, follow the recipe for Chantilly cream on page 19 then transfer to a piping bag.

Pipe the cream onto the lower part of the cranberry tart and serve. (If you find the flavour of cranberries too strong, you can make this recipe using cherries instead.)

POMEGRANATE – MERINGUE

Base 1 × quantity French meringue (page 19)

Colour topping seeds from 1 pomegranate

White topping 150 ml (5 fl oz) chilled cream

To make the base, follow the recipe for French meringue on page 19.

To make the white topping, beat the cream using an electric mixer until firm peaks form.

Spread the cream onto the meringue and arrange the pomegranate seeds on the upper part.

VIOLET – MERINGUE

Base 2 quantities French meringue (page 19)

Colour topping blue food dye | red food dye
a few pieces of violet candy

To make the base, follow the recipe for French meringue on page 19, but reserve half the beaten meringue before spreading the remaining mixture onto the tray to bake.

To make the colour topping, add a few drops each of the blue and red food dye to the reserved meringue, and mix to make a violet colour. Transfer to a piping bag fitted with a large nozzle, and pipe lines of meringue onto a tray lined with baking paper. Bake both trays of meringue for 2 hours, until the meringue lifts easily from the baking paper. Set aside to cool completely.

Carefully crumble the violet-coloured meringue over the upper part of the base. Decorate with a few pieces of violet candy.

BLUEBERRY – MERINGUE

Base 1 × quantity Shortcrust pastry (page 17)

Colour topping 200 g (7 oz) blueberries | 30 g (1 oz) sugar

White topping 1 × quantity Italian meringue (page 19)

To make the base, follow the recipe for Shortcrust pastry on page 17, but do not bake. Preheat oven to 180°C (350°F).

Arrange the blueberries onto the upper part of the chilled pastry and sprinkle with sugar. Bake for 20 minutes then set aside to cool.

To make the white topping, follow the recipe for Italian meringue on page 19 then transfer to a piping bag.

Pipe the meringue onto the lower half of the pastry rectangles. If desired, lightly brown the meringue with a small blowtorch before serving.

WHITE CHOCOLATE – COCONUT

Base 1 × quantity Shortcrust pastry (page 17)

Colour topping 200 ml (7 fl oz) coconut milk
150 g (5½ oz) white chocolate | blue food dye
250 ml (8½ fl oz) chilled cream | blue candies, to decorate

White topping 10 g (¼ oz) desiccated (shredded) coconut

To make the base, follow the recipe for Shortcrust pastry on page 17.

To make the coloured topping, heat the coconut milk and white chocolate together in a saucepan over low heat, stirring occasionally until the chocolate has melted. Allow to cool completely. Pour one third of the mixture into a small bowl and set aside. Add a few drops of blue food dye to the remaining mixture. Beat the cream with an electric mixer until firm peaks form. Fold two-thirds of the cream into the blue chocolate mixture and refrigerate for at least 2 hours.

To make the white topping, fold the remaining whipped cream into the reserved chocolate mixture. Stir in the desiccated coconut and refrigerate for at least 2 hours.

Place the blue mixture into a piping bag and pipe onto the upper part of the base. Spread the white mixture onto the lower part and decorate the tart with blue candies.

CURACAO – MERINGUE

Base 2 × quantity French meringue (page 19) | blue food dye

Colour topping | 20 ml (¾ fl oz) blue curacao
1½ teaspoons gelatine powder | 3 tablespoons blueberry jam

White topping 150 ml (5 fl oz) cream
2 teaspoons icing (confectioners') sugar

To make the base, follow the recipe for French meringue on page 17, but set aside half of the beaten meringue before spreading the remaining mixture onto the tray to bake. To the reserved meringue, add a few drops of the blue food colouring, and mix gently. Transfer to a piping bag fitted with a large nozzle, and pipe lines of meringue onto a tray lined with baking paper. Bake both trays of meringue for 2 hours, until the meringue lifts easily from the baking paper. Set aside to cool completely.

To make the colour topping, combine the curaçao and gelatine with 20 ml (¾ fl oz) water in a small saucepan over medium heat. Bring to the boil then pour the liquid onto a dinner plate and refrigerate until set. Cut the jelly into small circles.

To make the white topping, beat the cream using an electric mixer until firm peaks form. Add the sugar and beat for a further few seconds until the sugar is well incorporated. Transfer to a piping bag.

Spread the blueberry jam on the upper part of the base and pipe the cream over the top. Snap the blue lines of meringue into varying lengths and arrange on top of the cream. Top with the circles of jelly.

MOJITO - CREAM

Base 50 g (1¾ oz) unsalted butter | 70 g (2½ oz) flour
70 g (2½ oz) sugar

Colour topping 250 ml (8½ fl oz) chilled cream
1½ tablespoons icing (confectioners') sugar
a few drops pepppermint essence | mint, to decorate

White topping finely grated zest and juice from 2 limes
1 tablespoon icing (confectioners') sugar
150 ml (5 fl oz) chilled cream

Preheat oven to 180°C (350°F). Line a tray with baking paper.

To make the crumble base, combine the butter, flour and sugar, and coarsely mix with your hands to make a crumble. Spread the crumble onto the prepared tray and bake for 15 minutes, or until browned.

To make the colour topping, beat the cream using an electric mixer until firm peaks form. Add the sugar and mint essence, and mix until well incorporated. Transfer to a piping bag and refrigerate until needed.

To make the white topping, heat the lime juice and sugar with 10 ml (¼ fl oz) water in a saucepan over medium–high heat. Bring to the boil and simmer for about 5 minutes, or until the liquid has reduced to a syrup. Set aside to cool. Beat the cream using an electric mixer until firm peaks form. Add the lime syrup and mix until the syrup is well incorporated.

On serving plates, form the crumble into two 11 cm × 14 cm (4¼ in x 5½ in) rectangles. Pipe the lime mixture onto the upper part of the rectangle, and spread the cream onto the lower part. Sprinkle with the lime zest and mint, and serve.

PISTACHIO - CHANTILLY

Base 2 sheets brick (Tunisian) pastry (see p 13)
10 g (¼ oz) unsalted butter, melted

Colour topping 100 g (3½ oz) unsalted butter, softened
80 g (2¾ oz) caster (superfine) sugar | 1½ teaspoons pistachio paste (see p 13)
2 egg yolks | 200 ml (7 fl oz) milk | 15 g (½ oz) cornflour (cornstarch)
25 g (1 oz) unsalted pistachios, finely chopped

White topping 150 ml (5 fl oz) chilled cream
1 tablespoon icing (confectioners') sugar

To make the colour topping, beat the butter with 50 g (1¾ oz) of the sugar and ½ teaspoon of the pistachio paste until well combined. Set aside in the refrigerator. Beat the egg yolks with the remaining sugar until creamy, then add the cornflour and remaining pistachio paste. Place the milk in a saucepan over medium–high heat and bring to the boil. Pour the hot milk slowly onto the eggs, mixing gently to combine. Return to the saucepan over low heat and stir gently until the mixture thickens. Set aside to cool completely. When cool, beat the milk mixture and the chilled butter mixture together using an electric mixer. Transfer to a piping bag and refrigerate until needed.

To make the base, preheat oven to 180°C (350°F) and line a tray with baking paper. Cut the pastry into four 11 cm × 14 cm (4¼ in × 5½ in) rectangles. Place onto the prepared tray and and brush with melted butter. Bake for 3–4 minutes, or until the pastry is golden.

To make the white topping, beat the cream using an electric mixer until firm peaks form. Sift the sugar into the cream and beat for a further few seconds until the sugar is well incorporated.

On serving plates, stack two sheets of pastry on each plate. Pipe the pistachio custard onto the upper part of the pastry and spread the cream on the lower part. Sprinkle with the chopped pistachios.

APPLE - CINNAMON

Base 4 egg yolks | 45 g (1½ oz) sugar | 200 ml (7 fl oz) milk
1 vanilla bean | 4 slices white bread | 20 g (¾ oz) unsalted butter

Colour topping 2 granny smith apples, thinly sliced
20 g (¾ oz) sugar

White topping 150 ml (5 fl oz) chilled cream
1 tablespoon icing (confectioners') sugar
1 teaspoon ground cinnamon

To make the white topping, beat the cream using an electric mixer until firm peaks form. Sift the sugar and cinnamon into the cream and beat for a further few seconds until well incorporated. Refrigerate until needed.

To make the French toast base, mix together the egg yolks, sugar and milk in a shallow bowl. Cut the vanilla bean lengthways, and scrape the seeds using the tip of the knife. Add the seeds and the bean to the bowl. Soak each slice of bread in the mixture for at least a minute. Heat the butter in a frying pan over medium heat. Fry the French toast, in batches, for 1 minute on each side until golden brown.

Arrange the sliced apple on the upper part of the base and sprinkle with sugar. Spread the cream on the lower part and serve.

CUCUMBER - TZATZIKI

Base 1 × quantity Salted parmesan pastry (page 17)

Colour topping ½ cucumber | salt and ground black pepper

White topping 2 tablespoons Greek-style yoghurt
salt and ground black pepper

To make the base, follow the recipe for Salted parmesan pastry on page 17.

To make the colour topping, peel the cucumber and cut about two-thirds of it into thin slices. Chop the remaining cucumber into small cubes.

To make the white topping, combine the yoghurt with the cubed cucumber and season with salt and pepper.

Arrange the cucumber slices on the upper part of the base and spread the yoghurt onto the lower part. Season with salt and pepper, and serve.

BROAD BEAN - GOAT'S CHEESE

Base ½ teaspoon instant dried yeast | 125 g (4½ oz) flour
½ teaspoon salt | 2 tablespoons olive oil

Colour topping 250 g (9 oz) podded broad (fava) beans
2 tablespoons olive oil | salt and ground black pepper

White topping 2 tablespoons crème fraîche or sour cream
80 g (2¾ oz) soft goat's cheese

To make the white topping, mash together the crème fraîche and goat's cheese.

To make the pizza dough base, combine the yeast with 20 ml (¾ fl oz) lukewarm water in a small bowl and set aside for 5 minutes, or until foamy. Place the flour in a large bowl and make a well in the middle. Add 50 ml (1¾ fl oz) lukewarm water and the salt, olive oil and the yeast mixture. Mix thoroughly, pulling the flour inwards. Work the dough by hand, adding a little more flour if necessary. Tip onto a floured work surface and knead the dough until smooth and elastic. Place in a lightly oiled mixing bowl and cover with a damp cloth. Leave to rest in a warm place for 1 hour, or until doubled in size. Preheat oven to 210°C (410°F). Roll the pizza dough out into 12 cm × 15 cm (4¾ in × 6 in) rectangles. Spread the goat's cheese mixture over the base and bake for 15 minutes.

To make the colour topping, cook the beans in salted boiling water for 3 minutes, or until tender. Drain. If the beans have a hard skin, remove after cooking. Heat the oil in a frying pan and sauté the beans for 1–2 minutes. Season with salt and pepper.

Arrange the beans on the upper part of the base and return to the oven for 5 minutes. Remove from the oven and add a little more goat's cheese mixture on the lower part, if desired.

PEA - BACON

Base 250 g (9 oz) fresh peas, plus extra to decorate
1 chicken stock (bouillon) cube | 1 egg | 50 g (1¾ oz) flour
1 teaspoon baking powder | 20 g (¾ oz) butter, melted

White topping 70 g (2½ oz) bacon | 150 ml (5 fl oz) cream

To make the white topping, cook the bacon in a frying pan over medium–high heat then drain on paper towel. Place the bacon with the cream in a saucepan and heat for 5 minutes on low. Set aside to cool completely, then refrigerate for two hours.

To make the base, preheat oven to 180°C (350°F). Grease and flour a 15 cm × 24 cm (6 in × 9½ in) baking dish. Bring a saucepan of salted water to the boil, add the stock cube and stir until dissolved. Add the peas and cook for 5 minutes. Drain, but reserve a little of the cooking water. Purée the peas in a blender or food processor, adding a little of the reserved cooking water to make a smooth mixture. Pass the purée through a sieve. Add the egg, flour, baking powder and butter and stir until smooth. Pour the mixture into the prepared baking dish and bake for 30 minutes. Remove from the oven and set aside to cool for 5 minutes. Turn the tart out of the baking dish and cut into two 11 cm × 14 cm (4¼ in × 5½ in) rectangles.

Meanwhile, strain the bacon cream and discard the bacon. Beat the cream using an electric mixer until firm peaks form. Spread the bacon cream over the lower part of the tart and decorate with fresh peas.

MATCHA - SUGAR

Base 180 g (6½ oz) sugar | 4 eggs | 80 g (2¾ oz) flour
1 teaspoon baking powder | 4 teaspoons matcha powder
125 g (4½ oz) unsalted butter, melted

Colour topping 1 teaspoon matcha powder

White topping 15 g (½ oz) icing (confectioners') sugar

To make the base, preheat oven to 180°C (350°F). Grease and flour a 15 cm × 24 cm (6 in × 9½ in) baking tin. Beat together the sugar and eggs. Add the flour, baking powder, matcha and melted butter, and mix well. Pour into the prepared pan and bake for 30 minutes, or until a knife inserted into the cake comes out clean. Remove from the oven and set aside to cool.

Turn the cake out of the baking tin and cut into two 11 cm × 14 cm (4¼ in × 5½ in) rectangles. Using a sheet of foil to mask the lower part of the cake, sprinkle the upper part with matcha using a fine sieve. Mask the upper part with the foil and sprinkle the lower part with icing sugar.

KIWI FRUIT - CHANTILLY

Base 1 × quantity Shortcrust pastry (page 17)

Colour topping 4 kiwi fruit, peeled and sliced

White topping 1 × quantity Chantilly cream (page 19)

To make the base, follow the recipe for Shortcrust pastry on page 17.

To make the white topping, follow the recipe for Chantilly cream on page 19.

Spread the cream over the entire surface of the base. Arrange the kiwi fruit on the upper part and serve.

ROCKET - FETA

Base 175 g (6 oz) rocket (arugula) | 1 tablespoon olive oil
3 eggs | 20 g (¾ oz) parmesan, grated
40 ml (1¼ fl oz) vegetable oil | 190 g (6½ oz) flour
1 teaspoon baking powder | salt and ground black pepper

White topping 100 g (3½ oz) feta

To make the base, preheat oven to 180°C (350°F). Grease and flour a baking tin that's about 15 cm × 24 cm (6 in × 9½ in). In a large saucepan of boiling salted water, cook the rocket for 2 minutes. Drain the rocket but reserve a little of the cooking water. Blend the rocket with the olive oil in a food processor, adding enough of the cooking water to make a smooth purée. Whisk together the eggs and parmesan, then add the vegetable oil, flour and baking powder, and season with salt and pepper. Pour into the prepared pan and bake for 30 minutes, or until a knife inserted comes out clean. Remove from the oven and set aside to cool.

To make the white topping, mash the feta with a fork to make a paste.

Turn the base out of the baking tin and cut into two 11 cm × 14 cm (4¼ in × 5½ in) rectangles. Spread some feta across the lower part of the base and serve.

BEEF - AIOLI

Base 2 large slices of bread, toasted | olive oil, for drizzling

Colour topping 150 g (5½ oz) sliced rare roast beef

White topping 4 garlic cloves, roughly chopped | 1 egg
60 ml (2 fl oz) olive oil | salt and ground black pepper
3 tablespoons crème fraîche or sour cream

To make the white topping, place the garlic in a food processor and process until smooth. Add the egg and process until combined. With the food processor running, add the olive oil in a thin, steady stream. Stop the food processor. Season with salt and pepper and stir in the crème fraîche.

To make the base, cut the toast into 11 cm × 14 cm (4¼ in × 5½ in) rectangles. Drizzle with a little olive oil.

Arrange the beef on the upper part of the base and spread the aioli on the lower part.

CHESTNUT - MERINGUE

Base 1 × quantity French meringue (page 19)

Colour topping 50 g (1¾ oz) sugar
150 g (5½ oz) tinned whole chestnuts
edible gold leaf, to decorate (optional)

White topping 1 × quantity Chantilly cream (page 19)

To make the base, follow the recipe for French meringue on page 19.

To make the colour topping, combine the sugar with 50 ml (1¾ fl oz) water over medium–high heat and simmer for about 10 minutes, or until reduced to a syrup. Set aside to cool completely. Pour the syrup into a food processor along with the chestnuts and process until smooth. Transfer to a piping bag and refrigerate until needed.

To make the white topping, follow the recipe for Chantilly cream on page 19.

Pipe the chestnut purée onto the upper part of the base and spread the cream onto the lower part. Decorate with a little gold leaf, if desired.

CARAMEL – PANNA COTTA

Base 1 × quantity Panna cotta (page 19)

Colour topping 95 g (3¼ oz) sugar | pinch of sea salt
45 g (1½ oz) unsalted butter | 70 ml (2¼ fl oz) cream
handful of hazelnuts, coarsely crushed
edible gold dust, for decorating

To make the base, follow the recipe for Panna cotta on page 19.

To make the colour topping, melt 75 g (2¾ oz) of the sugar in a heavy-based saucepan over medium–high heat. When the sugar begins to colour, add the salt and butter, and stir to combine. Remove from the heat and stir in the cream. Refrigerate until needed. Line a tray with baking paper. Melt the remaining sugar in a small heavy-based saucepan over medium–high heat. When the sugar begins to colour, add the hazelnuts. Stir, then pour the mixture out onto the prepared tray. Set aside to cool then crush into small pieces. Sprinkle with a little gold dust.

Spread the caramel on the upper part of the panna cotta and sprinkle with the caramelised hazelnuts and sea salt.

DARK CHOCOLATE - WHITE CHOCOLATE

Base ½ × quantity Chocolate shortcrust pasty (page 17)

Colour topping 100 g (3½ oz) chocolate
edible gold dust, to decorate (optional)

White topping 200 ml (6¾ fl oz) coconut milk
150 g (1¾ oz) white chocolate | 150 ml (5 fl oz) cream
10 g (¼ oz) desiccated (shredded) coconut

To make the base, follow the recipe for Chocolate shortcrust pastry on page 17.

To make the colour topping, line a tray with baking paper. Place the chocolate in a heatproof bowl placed over a large saucepan of simmering water. Stir occasionally until the chocolate has completely melted then pour onto the prepared tray and spread into a smooth thin layer using a spatula. Refrigerate until the chocolate has set.

To make the white topping, heat the coconut milk and white chocolate together in a saucepan over low heat, stirring occasionally until the chocolate has melted. Allow to cool completely. Beat the cream with an electric mixer until firm peaks form. Fold the cream and the desiccated coconut into the chocolate mixture. Transfer to a piping bag and refrigerate for at least two hours.

Break the set chocolate into squares and place on the upper part of the base. Brush with a little gold dust to decorate, if desired. Pipe the coconut cream onto the lower part of the base and serve.

DARK CHOCOLATE - COCONUT

Base 200 g (7 oz) desiccated (shredded) coconut
400 g (14½ oz) condensed milk

Colour topping 200 g (7 oz) dark chocolate

To make the coconut base, combine the coconut with the condensed milk and refrigerate for 8 hours or overnight. Spoon into two 11 cm × 14 cm (4¼ in × 5½ in) rectangular moulds and return to the refrigerator.

To make the colour topping, melt the chocolate in a heatproof bowl placed over a large saucepan of simmering water.

Spoon the melted chocolate over the upper part of the base and serve.

MILK CHOCOLATE - WHITE CHOCOLATE

Base ½ × quantity Chocolate shortcrust pastry (page 17)

Colour topping 330 g (11½ oz) milk chocolate | 6 eggs, separated
grated dark chocolate, to decorate

White topping 150 g (5½ oz) white chocolate

To make the base, follow the recipe for Chocolate shortcrust pastry on page 17.

To make the white topping, line a tray with baking paper. Place the chocolate in a heatproof bowl placed over a saucepan of simmering water. Stir occasionally until the chocolate has melted, then pour onto the tray and spread into a thin layer. Refrigerate until the chocolate has set.

To make the colour topping, place 180 g (6½ oz) of the milk chocolate in a heatproof bowl placed over a large saucepan of simmering water. Stir occasionally until the chocolate has melted then remove from the heat and mix in the egg yolks. Using an electric mixer, beat the egg whites until stiff peaks form. Gently fold the beaten egg whites into the chocolate mixture then refrigerate for at least 2 hours. Melt the remaining milk chocolate in a heatproof bowl placed over a large saucepan of simmering water. Pour the melted chocolate into a 24 half-sphere chocolate mould, putting just a little chocolate into each mould then moving the mould about so that the chocolate thinly coats the mould. Place the mould in the freezer.

Transfer the chocolate mousse to a piping bag. Unmould the chocolate cups and fill each one with a little chocolate mousse. Arrange the filled cups on the upper part of the base and break a piece of the white chocolate to cover the lower part. Grate a little dark chocolate over the top to decorate.

BLACKBERRY - CHANTILLY

Base 1 × quantity Shortcrust pastry (page 17)

Colour topping 350 g (12½ oz) blackberries
1 tablespoon sugar (optional)

White topping 1 × quantity Chantilly cream (page 19)

To make the base, follow the recipe for Shortcrust pastry on page 17.

To make the white topping, follow the recipe for Chantilly cream on page 19.

Arrange the blackberries on the upper part of the base and spread the cream on the lower part. If desired, sprinkle the blackberries with a little sugar.